MADRIGALIA

MADRIGALIA

NEW & SELECTED POEMS

LISA RUSS SPAAR

A KAREN & MICHAEL BRAZILLER BOOK
PERSEA BOOKS / NEW YORK

Thank you to the editors of the following journals, in which new poems in this book first appeared, sometimes in a different version or with an alternate title.

Adroit Journal: "Heath," "Pastoral"; *Arkansas International*: "Lady Bird Taint"; *The Big Other*: "Spring Onion"; *Crazyhorse*: "Persimmon," "Wounded Vulture"; *Five Points*: "Ruby-Crowned Kinglet"; *The Harvard Review*: "Gradual," "Perseid"; *IMAGE: Art, Faith, Mystery*: "Estival"; *The Kenyon Review*: "Wasp"; *Letters Journal: Literature, Art, Spirit*: "Holy Week"; *Literary Imagination*: "Bachesque," "Columbarium," "Last Rose"; *The Los Angeles Review of Books Quarterly*: "Heavenly"; *On the Seawall*: "Breughelian," "Great-Horned Owls"; *The New Yorker*: "Sub Rosa"; *Ninth Letter*: "Debussy," "Vin Blank"; *Orion*: "Wild Strawberry"; *Pleiades*: "Adolescence"; *Plume*: "Oyster"; *Porter House Review*: "Nest," "Music Box"; *Shenandoah*: "Mantis"; *Virginia Quarterly Review*: "Bill Evansesque," "Magnolia Cone," "You Better Think"; *Yale Review*: "Torso"

The poems originally appearing in *Glass Town* are reprinted by the kind permission of Red Hen Press.

Persea Books, Inc.
90 Broad Street
New York, New York 10004

Library of Congress Cataloging-in-Publication Data

Names: Spaar, Lisa Russ, author.
Title: Madrigalia : new & selected poems / Lisa Russ Spaar.
Description: New York : Persea Books, [2021] | "A Karen & Michael Braziller book" | Summary:
    "A career-spanning volume by poet Lisa Russ Spaar, including new poems and selections
    from her previous poetry collections"—Provided by publisher.
Identifiers: LCCN 2021032136 | ISBN 9780892555369 (paperback ; acid-free paper)
Subjects: LCGFT: Poetry.
Classification: LCC PS3568.U7644 M33 2021 | DDC 811/.54—dc23
LC record available at https://lccn.loc.gov/2021032136

Book design and composition by Rita Lascaro
Typeset in Charter
Manufactured in the United States of America. Printed on acid-free paper.

ACKNOWLEDGMENTS

I am beyond fortunate, over the many years of writing represented by the poems in this collection, to have had the support of my gifted and much-admired colleagues, friends, and students in the Creative Writing Program and the Department of English at the University of Virginia. I owe a debt, as well, to a host of administrators and deans in the College of Arts & Sciences. I received invaluable assistance during this period from a Guggenheim Fellowship in Poetry; the Rona Jaffe Foundation's Award for Emerging Women Writers; a Library of Virginia Poetry Award; the Carole Weinstein Poetry Prize; a Jefferson Scholars Foundation Faculty Award; two Arts, Humanities, and Social Sciences Research grants from the College of Arts & Sciences at UVA; and a Horace W. Goldsmith NEH Distinguished Teaching Professorship.

I offer special thanks to my friends at Baylor University, where for the past three years I've had the privilege of serving as Beall Visiting Poet. It was with this inspiring, welcoming, and generous community of scholars, students, and writers that many of the madrigals were first shared.

My deep and abiding gratitude, always, to Karen and Michael Braziller and all of the Persea family, and especially to my brilliant editor of seventeen years, Gabriel Fried.

My three children and my students have been my steadfast teachers. This book is dedicated to them, and to Rosemary Yoko and Eleanor Violet (Evie), brand new to the world and already full of music and wisdom.

CONTENTS

from GLASS TOWN (1999)

NEW POEMS: THE MADRIGALS

madrigal (n.)

"short love poem," especially one suitable for music, also "part-song for three or more voices," 1580s, from Italian *madrigale*, which is of uncertain origin; probably from Venetian dialect *madregal* "simple, ingenuous," from Late Latin *matricalis* "invented, original," literally "of or from the womb," from *matrix* (genitive matricis) "womb"

Online Etymology Dictionary

ADOLESCENCE

Lindens in a novel were what
I wanted to be under, angsty & fey
beside the quay I'd learned
to pronounce as key,

as I knew to say Yeats,
not Yeets. The clatter of wheels
I craved was just my rib-corseted
heart that only special hands might heal.

Blame in the virulent jaundice
of that autumn. Brutal shiver
to school on suburban sidewalks,
lugging hunger privileged

as a heavy book. I dreamed you even then,
above my breasts, undreamed-of-plot, without an end.

BACHESQUE

Mired in this baroque, sonic nave,
long ago reduced to briared staves

revived again, again, again by hair
& gut, is there room for air,

for me, the grief I keep at bay, dull,
dormant as the season's huddle?

Symptom of illness or oblivion,
enough of this abstraction.

I know my soul most in indigo
tureen of dusk, delta of still-bare oaks,

sycamores, & how do I know
what else might wish for extended arms

in which a visitor might, exhausted
by the fever of this counterpoint, alight?

BAPTIST

See him, shoulders clapping
through clabberous mountain

laurel, snoot deep now in stand
of fleur-blistered twigs bent

to mouth, suckling buds honeyed
& rush-tainted as a pearl-breasted,

flushed necklace of young quail
trailing ankles over an old-timey grave's

wind-rocked, periwinkle sky,
nor does he shy from a quick lie-down

in the grassy mattress, patient beside
the creek's babbling stripe, a bridegroom,

as he came, husks of shirt & more
bathed in what he was made for.

BILL EVANSESQUE

Quartal voicings, the alcohol.
Swallows in a martini sky, jig-sawed

glassware, velvet-filleted pine trees,
brilliance & nada in cascade antipodes,

lightly side-stepping with motivic arches
the oiled train trestles, corner bars,

& township caul of natal New Jersey,
the Ampex taping genius, its privacies

reel to reel, capturing the bass taking
the low down, suppressed twinge

of truth, reefer, junk, as winter south-pawed
in, despite all. Nights playing a show

one-handed, virtuosic, after a needle hit
a nerve. In tones variceal. Lyric. Cirrhotic.

BIRD IN THE HOSPITAL

Glassed-in atrium walkway from clinics
to cafeteria, today transformed to souk,

kiosks of cheap scarves, nickel wrist cuffs,
rings, tote bags for sale to tired nurses, scrubs,

patients, families in denial, fatigue, so many
reasons to pay for what diverts. I'm seeking coffee,

escape from me within this infected theater
of What's-at-Stake, so at first I think retinal floater,

mistake, bit of code gone rogue, throating
lamp fixture, high sill. She sees it too, girl arching

in her wheeled chair, face a fallen moon,
limbs deflated, albumen eyes aflare with the amphetamine

of this taunt scythe whooshing over us,
wee cross doubled in the unblinking thunder of her irises.

BREUGHELIAN

Winter, The Birdtrap, Pieter Brueghel II

A matter of low countries—
ice-stunned canals, dusk-cheeky

planks scalloped with steaming bowls,
skates, a scape theatrical & claustrophobic—

multifarious concoction on view
but intimate too, woman with hiked wool

skirt peeing in snow, old shed door
propped up, rigged with trick stick to trip & floor

unwitting doves: scant meat, true.
Doll bones. Steep rooftop snoods,

black trees, vista latticed, un-baited,
single black crow bearing the weight

of thought, pre-modern, anachronistic.
So already slaughtered, I know myself in it.

COLUMBARIUM

At a dovecote outside London
my whole hand just fit inside
one of the many open-ended slots.
Easy, guide said, *for pigeons*

unwittingly to roost, & the cook
to pluck one out for roasting!
Withdrawn, my palm thrummed
electrically, guiltily, as today

touching your vault in a wall
of funereal apartments. False spring
spurred me, muddy shoes, compost,
a racket like the wind that held the smoke

unbandaging all of you but bone scree—
you never interred in just one body.

COURTESAN

> ...*as though to protect*
> *What it advertises.*
> John Ashbery, "Self-Portrait in a Convex Mirror"

Body is a temple, but who can read inside it?
Beneath sheets, a girl, flashlight pressed to palm:
that flanged red ghost deafened cicadas, traffic qualm,
with nervous, ungrateful hue. Is captured light

the subject, then? Or dark. Let in too much
& it's the anti-lyric—obscurity galore.
Too little? Don't bother to be born.
Light, meet Dark, in this intricate brocade

of sky freighting the stream, summer's obi,
consciousness unraveling the heart's claim.
Wade there, water-bird precarious, a drinking game.
Lift slowly the drape of consonants.

Reveal your vowels. Not all of them. Arouse
the polluted miraculous water that we house.

DEBUSSY

Sunburnt at the bench, bent note
concussing summer behind black moats,

yard copses, carport, my lesson's context,
metronome obelisk tocking *practice, practice,*

to the tune of a scorching supper casserole.
Matte pages of the Elkan-Vogel

Claire de Lune spread, so way beyond me,
paraphs, chords stacked as cinders, key-

holes intricate, abstract, impassable:
pedal points subtle, untranslatable

as sand in a bathing suit crotch, sheet music
fingers whispering buttons, a blouse,

seams of my girlhood mute, fidgety,
milliseconds already splitting into other entities—

ESTIVAL

"islanded with sunshine"
                    Dorothy Wordsworth

Nothing quite rhymes like time
to kill and this long, clingstone schooling—
reason traitorous, the season a bomb
of decoy mimosa, bird-curtsy, the pool

under-shattering low leaves, God
saying *now*. I'm not sure
I'll ever be ready. Will I go easy,
nail from a weathered board, splinter

pulled from a foot surprised & bare
as I came, legs wrapped around—?
Love trumps pain is the lesson with which
I'm out of my mind. The sun's going down

slow, in our language. I thank its freighted skull.
As though any other life were possible.

GRADUAL

Does God create desire so we'll loathe
the aging body for its hold on us,
or does desire create God to hold
all that wanting one another sows in us?

Either way, Wonder, let's go slow
as we can, closing in, while not forgetting
the generous pour of Time's bartender,
the one with the heavy hand, forgotten,

whose liquid sutures eventually dissolve
even the children we once were, like *love*
held in *dissolve*, the disappearing décolletage
of gravity-driven sand. Perhaps when love

is greatest, we do die, into whatever
our bodies were: swamp, cell walls, travellers.

GREAT HORNED OWLS

Over winter's pit, orchestral tune-up
of settle & unrest, un-tuxedoed,
comes her dactylic *whooooo, ooo, ooo,*
rum, unorthodox, muezzin hiccup

whose source I'm always searching out
inside a camouflaged theater, gray scrim
tangle, kudzu, ivy opera cloaks, pines,
a mistletoe-gibbeted dead oak.

High up, she's there! sturdy as a contract,
ruthless satellite, cat's ears, head swiveling.
From eave above my window, in answer,
another winged span swoops, alights upon her back.

As in a mirror, two bodies make one
new thing. Silence then. Blenched, unharrowing.

HAPPY

The hap in it, sure. The stance.
The happen, the *circum-*, the chance

that unknown neighbors I can't see
beyond a bamboo moat play this evening,

on repeat, *I'm in love with your body*.
Baaah-deeeaahh is how they confess, in harmony,

a full 20 minutes so far & the only lyric,
synthy as the pollen-taxed air, a phrase carsick,

sultry as my fever. What else is there
to say? A swarming starling choir

raises the star-struck banner of its kingdom
over the grill-smoked subdivision,

the wild cherry's hashish blooms, malaise
undone, & okay, I am. What the song—what its title—says.

HEATH

Brontë Parsonage

It calls to me, right out of girldom—
no rights, part fiction—

though once, adult, with bread husk
& styrofoam cup of tea, I trespassed

in unrequite through its stone ways,
heather blacker than the gorse, salt hay,

took refuge from wind's heart-toss
in a divot, tawny loam, green mosses,

hares slipping silent in & out of wells,
thinking: this is how they survived, quelling

the house, hour-shackle, self's capsize
in repast of linnets, curlew, sky's

knives: stream & beck filleting underfoot,
its silver mouth—sought, untitled, you.

HEAVENLY

Scuttle moon,
I lick thee.

How far we've come,
even when I've slept

through your scythe,
your skull & priestly dome,

your going dark,
the sky all ark.

All the ways
you've tried to show

me how it's going to go.
I project, & yet

it's true, your hold.
I look. My eyes burn gold.

HOLY WEEK

Every evening now, the geese.
I wish it meant something
more than shit-sludged pond
beside the local nursing home,

denial's last resort, Our Lady
of Glacial Melting. I'm falling,
as I always pray to do, in derangement
of blossom-prosper, for you,

pined for, prior even to Saturnalian,
suspended nowhere-tilt of amnion.
Believe me. Or don't. I could not cast
words more true, us, once suckling

the calving ice of mother's milk,
pale as first light, magnetic blue as flight.

LADY BIRD TAINT

In the derring-do capes of Hallowe'en
or fidgety fairy tale widow weeds,

in masses they ribbon windows, trunks,
the south side of anything, bargaining,

bustling, as diapausal days commence
& paper-thin frost locks down the lawn.

What penultimate forces drove my mother,
demented, to speak, on her last day, a blurry,

exhausting scatter-flock of sense? Who can say?
How do we get as far as we do, astray

as these spotted garnet beetles, black masked,
infiltrating even the hair's-breadth cracks of casks,

bladder presses, winery batches lost forever
to notes of rancid butter, instinct, cankered dearth?

LAST ROSE

What gives meaning work to do?
This rabbit, drowned in winter pool,

fetal, soaked sweater sock-body
bumping the filter? Or these fait accompli

cardboard boxes a dead friend's
grown children pack with panic?

Deep calls to deep, they say.
Yet sleep won't come. And in the vase

that holds a stem I stole,
water's shallow drink is gone

to sky from whence it came.
And love? Must it stay, unable

to travel where we finally go? What gives
work meaning? Perhaps if I could rest, I'd know.

LITERATURE

While I nod off—eyeglasses & lamp
still lit, mouth spittled, neck cramped—

the detective in my novel drowns
or is shot or runs off with who done it,

if she's not herself the killer.
Does it matter if she's gone chill,

changed her mind, race, uses a pronoun
that might some one offend—

or that I slept through her last meal,
didn't care enough to stay awake to see?

I'm using this word loosely, I know—
"literature." I'm using her, too, folio

distraction, finger in the dyke of my insomnia,
bodybag zipped to chin, deep-sixed in oblivion.

MAGNOLIA CONE

Primitive angiosperm, genus
prior even to bees,

autumn's also my tongue,
gossamer-threaded spindle

of ovarian fire set amidst leathery
tepals. How survive eons

of earth's glacial mow, torrid grist,
thus exposed? Follicled fist,

carpeled blason seed-clits cajoled
toward split & go, O, Magnol,

French botanist, more than the cake-
like petal flesh of summer, so redol, so thick

it whets, these swollen spears
make me mourn the life I'll leave.

MAKE-UP

As old as civilization, the need to stain,
to paint the lips with currants crushed, the skin
preserved in resin, beeswax, arsenic.
Warm rosewater. Bird lime. Swipes of kohl,

from the Arabic *al-kuhul*, thus "alcohol,"
spirit sublimated from powder at great expense
for fear, for wrinkles. Gum of frankincense.
Is any of this different from a lover's lie,

however loving, however white, well meant,
I've nothing planned, all is well, the gentle foam
of the hard unsaid: I'm returning to my home.
My neuroses make me want to run away,

as in *mascara*—from mask, buffoon. These dyes
turn tears to toxic rivers. But losing you? I'd rather die.

MANTIS

Earth's heir, pre-historic prophet
in prayerful ambush position
on the sea side of this beach-house door,
intricate erector-set contraption

of twigs camouflaged to match
salt-bitten boards, you swivel
your skeptical, bicycle-seat head
my way, a cosmos horoscopal

in eyes bulbous as convex mirrors.
I see myself, prey to the cri de coeur
of visitations. But you're no augur;
I'm on my way to the outdoor shower.

I know in sex you'll eat your mate. In hunger,
your self, as at my hackled back, you always stir.

MUSIC BOX

A wrist of sticks cut, thrust in water
to force the sweet crease of cherry flosses
& then forgotten now thickens with fur-dross,
greeny on the windowsill through which a neighbor's

radio opines in Friday-night nostalgia
to the tune of a six-pack of something.
A tired story, Romance: On such an Evening,
&c, the Light—unhinged by sudden thaw,

the wind dovetailing through strappy trees
its clarity, its eyeblink—bringing to the darkened
space of a heart-fisted ribcage a fresh chance.
Lift the lid, unbend the stiff, sprung figure

of speech within, tutu spread like the spirit's bloom
ringing hope's vase with the snow of freedom.

NARCISSUS

Whatever these once were— dissolved tree
roots, discarded plate, or just dog bones buried

in the yard, this Neapolitan eruption
of yellow balconette & frilly AA-cups

nods on emerald scapes above a puddle.
Like adolescent girls, they tend to huddle,

numb, narcotic. Despite their cliques,
I love them so, each one unique

& on this chilly morning, just hanging on
for quick wink despite sun's certain shovel

ready to stir up all things pelvic.
Image to take mostly figuratively. Tricky,

how even these spathed blooms read as erotic.
See them sigh as one, believing this mere rhetoric.

NEST

What confidence, instinct,
O Precarious, made this wattled brink

of botched starts, breasted lore,
whose thatch in the fork

of two branches, shows—duh—
the first home: pubis, mother,

me. In my dream-code,
it's to this contrived abode,

coda to the flits of love,
& bossed by laws inter-woven

as the center of a universe—
feed, fleece, fly—that I return.

Life's a parsing of the verb *to hide*,
to run from any public place to what's inside.

NOVEMBER

Frost-whiskered lawn,
pink creep of dawn
pinching tree-bones:
ransom note I open alone

on the landing,
a lifted-harness cling,
humic fissure, dread,
that this scribble of espresso

will not allay.
In my last dream, I saved
my children. Woke. Wept hard,
arms strapped, crossing guard,

to chest. I was mother, then, not citizen.
Why would I fall to sleep again?

OYSTER

Consider the closed & frigid oyster,
promiscuous sea's non sequitur:

speechless purse, close hidden tongue.
A primitive tool, a cancerous lung,

cask of milky silks & erstwhile pearl
of inmost unable, like a girl,

unfinished, ugly, one might say, or pure.
Yet on a wintry night, a cure.

Who would say "ugly" to any girl?
How be too pure? Yet what is true unfurls

at the bone-thin, crenellated curl
as edge jiggles apart, like death, surly

at first and then, with a crack, sigh, life
drips again to zest from knife.

PASTORAL

New Jersey, 1970

In retrospect was it heaven,
pink gasses sundowning over Rt. 287?

Even a stricken state can be true spouse
to one thing: not the old homestead outhouses,

later stoked with bags of pesticides,
but the splintered hole, where, days, midnights,

an equalizing flux & metabolis
of seated humans emptied body to abyss.

What is nature now? Too old to know,
too young to say. In drawers, cabinets, lie stones

unearthed—arrowhead, grinding—by plow-blades
foot-driven by people moved to save

a history not theirs to share. Road kill
this morning, red as pox. As evening's spill.

PERSEID

We're always awake, but they never fall
for us, nor allow us to see their stone-iron
gassy spectra & debris trails bruiting the dark
as a cosmic x-ray of our pelvic secrets.

What still stands at the end of sex?
Is it our own demise, in which, Freud opines,
we put off & off believing? Why?
Is it the way a wary child protects a parent,

hiding all it really knows? And life
just an expanse of field, a torched textual gloss,
a humid summer foyer we expect across?
Let's not know our last days as our last. And this

is how you'll know me, after I'm erased.
In any place you are, I'll wear your face.

PERSIMMON

As a word make-believes
the world it stops,
so these cirrhotic fruits
dropped, boozy, in the grass,

conjure that crone yesterday
in line clutching paperbacks,
Joan of Arc, Galileo, hair matted in patches,
mis-matched sneakers, skirt of urine,

muttering "he won't like it, he won't,
you're not my friend." Dead mother
revived in schizophasia astringent as pap burr
so ripe the black calyx leaves

its canker stamp on my tongue.
Meaning's address? Far, far-flung.

POSTHUMOUS

Mot-made-flesh, how, still
made of words, can I
know, will I, when I'm, will
it be as it once was, body all

around me, gills, no apart,
fed through the belly in a yoke
of seawater, blue heart,
sepal lungs, world I impart,

doubled, when you are blown
inside me now. Is that how?
Wind as muse swelling red moan
of maples, vestigial tailbone

of thought making of every again
we did not refuse a heaven?

RUBY-CROWNED KINGLET

for my father

Not entirely at peace, his trouble's
not with these undredged gutters

needing swiping. Eight decades as the chute
to death may be what he delays by doing.

Yet still so sharp & quick, he doesn't miss
the kit, small as his long-ago boyhood fist,

warbler greeny with white eye ring
on nearby branch. A wren?

In aggressed arousal, or homage,
it tilts its head, as if to show the crimson spot,

give the old man an ID, or could it be
a fleet recognition of shared intransigence,

the risk, the bow, the going forth,
wee chariot heart, singing north.

SPRING ONION

We'd taste their tender woods
in the milk of mother, goat, cow, if we could.

I'm wet for them, erect lashes,
emerald fans rising from dead grass,

minute pearl bulbs below, hairy; tubular bundles
above, fresh, *young*, a word hung

in the throat, like stung, or lung.
More winter leek now than sprung

anew, than upside-down brooms,
vernal strops Persian Jews once used

to strike one another at Passover,
I gather them like clover,

still slave to whet, to beginning's urge.
My penance to adore their Lenten scourge.

SUB ROSA

I know time lives in me
& not the other way around.
Many mornings it wants out,
silver crevasses round the eyes.

Or in corpse of midnight, also,
picking poor heart's padlock, spending...
but wait.—What does it mean to *spend*
the days that you are flown

if I believe time lives in us, & not
the other way around? Clippers
in hand beneath an iron arbor,
wielding insect spray, I pause

in a bower that has blown with eros.
I mean roses. Fresh as flesh. What time is.

SURGICAL

Is it migratory instinct that wakes me
at 3 am, moon canthus to canthus
in unsynoptic glare? I'm sick, you see.
I'm ruttish for thee. See for yourself

is what "autopsy" means. Operate
as April's aneurysm disturbs this line,
these very words a mind-muddle, irate
as tea leaves. Read me. Read me. Read me.

Which is another way of saying "cut," or love
the folded pages stitched by pain.
Tell me true. Which word in what's above
to you is most transparent? Is it *is*?

I hope it's love. Spend it with your eyes.
Lick its change. Anatomize its prize.

TORSO

I admit I pine for it, the belly vulnerable
& all that goes with that pagoda hall,
shoulder to hips, a sweet disclose of brute
my nose traces like stock lineage to its root.

Torso whose root is in the Latin "thyrsus,"
stalk, trunk, so in my night-dreams vegetus,
obviously a tree is never just a tree.
Why should this matter to anyone but me,

except the heart it houses feeds a watershed.
Not just literally. *Please, watch your head*
I might say to myself (mentally tracing the route
I've just conjured), not just for me, resolute,

displaced by lust, but for you, those my love
for him forgets, hymning the altar I hover above.

VIN BLANK

Is elsewhere just a concept,
or is my love, elsewhere,
the concept: vacant stare,
horizon's brief reception

of a sun that can't know
it's seen as sinking. Sunk.
I admit I'm drinking. But not drunk.
The way a face trembles in a floe

of melting snow, is all.
A wavering that might as well
be caused by tears as vitriol.
It's stepping through the wall—

the audience startled. Then stunned.
A rogue star on the move, as though done.

WASP

Corseted, dandle-legged, as cold
comes on, you, isolato, bumble over

this room, ziggurating blind-slats
& bookshelves, dive-bombing

the lampshade, falling flat,
quiet, seeking. . . . egress?—what?

Having crept up from Jurassic myrrh
through Vivaldi's four seasons,

I know you, parasitontal, will outlast
my dread. But dread of what?

Anti-social or lost, I love
your company, as, today, love

hung above my body, its ah
of summer, autumn far off, a rogue coda.

WILD STRAWBERRY

Cinquefoil heaven behind tract homes,
creeping with emerald mouse-tail vines

& jujube seeded garnet thimbles,
you grew beside the place we buried

goldfish, caged mice, the small pets
we were permitted, first deaths

wrapped in toilet tissue, tucked
into metal bandage boxes

the size of packs of cigarettes
we later smoked in that field, too tufted

to let us dig deep, not that we could,
skinny arms, toy trowels. Alone

I crouched, neck freckling, seared,
plastered with radiance, with interfere—

WHOLE FOODS

Harvest's a concept of inside
fluorescence versus this outside

concrete apron, baskets stoked, pinecones
doused in cinnamon, chrysanthemums,

hormonal gourds arrayed on bleachers
in plastic pots. No preaching.

I'll go in for organic apples, my milk of soy.
But last week, beneath glassy evening sky,

Conestoga clouds rushing westward-ho,
I helped my father clear his little plot,

sour-mash cornstalk stubble underfoot,
a pelvic register of scythe, of lost output

that knows the measure of a bushel, a weather vane.
Or barrow of dug-up potatoes, rotted by rain.

WOLF SPIDER

Nothing lurk or shy
about its march today

from the rank culvert
of a winter boot shaft.

How long in that shearling
empty footbed, closeted

three seasons? Not long,
I'm guessing, hoping,

thinking miniscule timebomb
egg sacs as the hours scrimp

on daylight, frost steals up, driving
the feral within. I relate. The bite

of ruffian wind makes me wild for him.
Naked inside clothes. Almost inhuman.

WOUNDED VULTURE

Wing-struck wretch, beaky plague-doctor
limping the yard's periphery
as the dog hurtles from couch to window,
maddened by proximity

to your miasmic sentience,
vapor of unhinged gland, entrail.
Slim pickings in the English Ivy:
foetal mice and voles, snails,

more cat-toys than carrion.
Dropped from the homing gyre,
what are we? The light's especially
spindly and sonic at this hour.

Do you hear it in the ether, helixical,
now that you yourself are felled?

YOU BETTER THINK

"Think," Aretha Franklin & Teddy White

This dive-bombing catbird
swoops low in divots, porchward,

firing her warning shot—
all adolescence, swift & raucous—

aimed at me. I've strayed too close
to her hidden, sloppy nest.

I've been her. Loading the dishwasher,
passive-aggressively shaking ass,

fists bristled with dinner party cutlery,
finger-scraping the plates of infidelity:

I've lip-synched to the Queen
of What You've Tried to do to me.

Me? I've lost the thinking gene.
I'm seventeen. A loaded magazine. Pure gasoline.

ZED

Orchard

Rhyme with me, you.
By which I mean my love
of vowels, their décolletage
that swells a progress

through the consonantal briars.
When I want to harm myself
I look at sky. I feel its push,
the *within* that blood, flesh,

only stitch around & through.
An instant to be something else:
a bomb or mate or nightmare,
at which fantasy excels.

Pip exposed is how I'll fly
when I'm mere fragrance, bye-and-bye.

from GLASS TOWN (1999)

HALLOWE'EN

On the night of skulled gourds,
of small, masked demons
begging at the door,
a man cradles his eldest daughter
in the family room. She's fourteen,
she's dying because she will not eat
anymore. The doorbell keeps ringing;
his wife gives the sweets away.
He rubs the scalp
through his girl's thin hair.
She sleeps. He does not know
what to do.
When the carved pumpkin
gutters in the windowglass,
his little son races through the room,
his black suit printed with bones
that glow in the dark.
His pillowsack bulges with candy,
and he yelps with joy.
The father wishes he were young.
He's afraid of the dream
she's burning back to,
his dream of her before her birth,
so pure, so perfect,
wth no body to impede her light.

ANOREXIA

I loathe the blade
that enters a body
in order that what is slaughtered
might be eaten,

but love the blade
held next to warm flesh,
reflecting what is still alive,

and carry the sharp edge close,
a cold locket
between my breasts,
a thin mirror
whittling away
at what remains over the bone—

but slowly,
so it might never be said, later,
that anything but love
ever existed between these two:
the blade, and the body.

RAPUNZEL'S GIRLHOOD

In the house where I lived
before the tower,
we kept a tub filled with carp,
sleek secrets cruising the black water,
orange as embers.
Their mouths were round as my wrist
and always pulsing for more
of the grain we fed them.
I have a mouth with no tongue
and I explored it in my room
as far as my fingers could reach.
For some reason, I'd close my eyes
when I did this,
and always I'd picture those fish,
circling stories below in their basin,
sometimes coming to the surface,
where I'd glimpse their large, wild eyes,
the fret of their flesh, elusive
as answers bobbing into view
in my Magic-8 Ball toy—
"Fat Chance" or "No Way"
and sometimes "It's in the Bag."
My lonely body asked my questions
for me—the dull ache of bones growing
overnight, of eggs preerupting inside me,
thimble breasts hot as coals—
and always the crone's hands filling
my bath, shearing my dress up,
testing the steam. It took two hands
for her to wrest a terrified fish,
pin it beneath her sodden knee,
slit its throat. I was always surprised
that something so hidden

could be exposed that way, the guts
coiled and glazed with musk,
little ladders of bones I'd prop
against the sill for the mice to climb—
and the meat I'd close my mouth around,
my tongue pressing all the remnants
of ocean echo down my throat
before I'd spit the tough flesh out.

INSOMNIA

If you pretend you are not alone,
or that you are well-born
and protected, then of course
you can go out and stand in the yard.
As you would do anything
you wanted to do.
But if you go out
like an adolescent in a car
on a back road,
like a suspicious farmer,
then you will feel the dark enter you.
Whatever roams the air tonight
comes anyway,
as your willful body rumbles on,
digesting and breathing
in spite of your rigid watchfulness.
Let the footfall outside the bedroom window
be your own.
Take the white road that burns
past what endures but cannot move.

A DOUBT

It's nothing, a mordent
of the spirit,
a small fall
like the exhalation
of a breath;
the way that,
for just a moment
after the ribcage sinks
in a house
where someone is dying,
there is a silence
so deep, it is impossible
to tell its source
or to believe
the beating,
a small, sharp scruple
in your own breast.

GLASS TOWN

1. E. Brontë: Last Hours

In one vertiginous moment,
she knew that her bones
and all the convoluted circuitry
that sat upon their throne
had turned to water.
Panting in the back passage,
her wrists sunk in an apron full
of raw meat joints,
even the dogs' anxious snuffling
at her skirts must now be held
in light esteem, her art
of starvation almost a moot point—
that rapture of weightless violence,
the inner work that had sustained her
when the "world was lost" to her,
but wasn't, really. Not yet.
Each tongue, each tooth of language
had held her here until this moment.

2. "Buried Alive": C. Brontë, Twilight

The house ticks with migrainous music—
on the landing, her father's clock taps
against its cabinet, its grimly rocking pendulums
mocking the opened front gate, the smocking
of Queen Anne's Lace and feverfew tangled there.
She's looking out through the taunting arbor
and beyond, across the broken orchard of headstones
in the churchyard, to the pocked wall of the tower,
into which her father has discharged his angry pistol

each dawn for twenty years.
This is the hour she should belong
to nothing, not the dark eyes
of potatoes she's flicked out
with Tabby's knife,
not the stoveblacking, not the lapful
of needlework: whipstitch, and blanket,
and chain. And not yet to the lines of black ink
she'll cast herself into later, Papa in bed at last—
still all inward darkness, I left
...about twilight... Is she thinking
of him, then, of her *master*, her Belgian *monsieur*,
the dank smoke of his cigar
among the espaliered quince of the parterre—
each scribbled admonishment in the margins
of her old school essays still a thrilling
garnish of hope? The wiry, faded copses
and brambles of his scrawled, off-hand remarks
she studies, throwing herself against them
repeatedly each day—in the absence
of real letters—though outside
birds throttle the dusk with song,
and her *sorrow touches none with pain*,
and, beyond her, through the steeply pitched,
shabby houses of the villagers, infested
and overworked, the cobbled road
passes, whiter as the dark descends.

3. C. Brontë, at the Sea: Burlington, 1838

Here, I'd hoped to feel
unpunishable and free—
my knotted self flung open
across an escapade so endless
even *my* eyes couldn't hold it—.

But now I see that even the sea
is governable, its relentless,
bidden cresting and tumbling,
its sigh of hurtled secrets.
Here, silence is turned to *tsk* and tears,

inside out and raw with depths.
No bather, I watch others
wade the sandflats, slick
with mystery, their naked, unsuitable feet
assaulted by the husk-strewn surf

and the terrible powers.
I watch—my lot—caught
in its invisible, cosmic staves,
vainly deciphering the semen spray,
the diminishing stone.

4. Writing *Jane Eyre*, Manchester, August 1846

Lover, crawl back to me
through these thorns,
a briery hedge of words erupting
in these rented rooms of enforced shadows

and silence, where my father lies,
felled and sleeping, his head swathed in bandages—
the ripe films that blinded his eyes
having been excised, and replaced with healing's
own dark dressing. The street outside
is somnolent with pavement
and dull, mechanical noise, and dusty,
shadeless trees. In here, the nurse
comes and goes, her basin wound with cloth
and witchhazel. I've ordered the meals,
mutton and tea. And, when I was asked
to do so, I was witness to the operation,
my father's eyes pried open, two murky orbs
that the knife's blade circled and unclouded.
My tooth aches, irksome reminder
of me. But see how far I've brought her,
my Jane? She has *as much soul as you—
and full as much heart*. Do you think
that your *stained truth* can go unpunished
in such tales? Go ahead, write
a shoemaker's address in the margin of my letter
before you tear it up. I'll have you.
But not before you wrestle through this barbed
kingdom of my making, and it thieves
those kindled eyes that measured me
by *mortal flesh* alone, and not before
you climb, fumbling your way along the walls
by touch, to this hot attic, arrested
in a feverish spell, where, my love,
I have not been sleeping.

5. T'Parson's Anne

"Anne's nothing, absolutely nothing"
C. Brontë, *My Angria and the Angrians*

This morning she would have me tear
the clothes from the bed we share, gasping
"the snow, the snow, I cannot bear
its weight," and, sure, her fingers gripping mine

seared, all chilblains, fever, ice.
Eager always to be going forward, away,
what pelting December storm was she mining,
dogged by duty, our mild disdain, and the barking,

tubercular cough that Ellen, who is with us,
ministers to with Gobbold's and carbonate of iron?
We are here at No. 2 Cliff, and outside
it's still May, Scarborough, the bay guiltless

as a glass of water. Yesterday, she would ride
upon the stony strand in a donkey cart,
all gray bird bones in a quilted pile,
nearly invisible but for the driver's tender fist

of a face and our own stricken masks,
walking beside her. Still, I tell you,
if one of us was born to bear the weighted task
of a man above, beside, beneath her,

it's this girl, our "dear little Anne,"
whose motion outshines my ire, and Emily's
paralyzing instinct, and Branwell's quick capitulation—
nearly all of us, now, shamed by Death.

Out of Haworth she took herself, and throve
a while without us, and out she would be carried
one last time, in Papa's arms, to the carriage that strove
to bear her here. And out of bed she rises now,

and will not let me fasten her waist
or move the chamber pot from beneath the bed.
She sits at the window by the sea, place
of the little lie she allowed herself,

drawing small, decided breaths
faithful as the waves below,
their small shoulders hunched,
an obliterating blizzard of flux and light.

6. Glass Town: A Childhood

Day sifted slowly, like sand, filled, and then tapered off
to an early, pointed stillness.
Always, the glass funnel of orphaned hours
hung, an empty womb above us—.

Night fed us—first with the haunted noise
of our mother's absent, asthmatic laboring,
silenced now, across the yard, beneath the heavy flags
of St. Michael's and All Angels.

We grew into this darkness,
clutching one another in bed, our hearts
skipping under a snow of covers that the oblivious
moon lit, crossed, and then abandoned.

We built—in our cramped, stark room—a kingdom
of Asiatic fronds and heaped-high banquets and grand,
prismatic, hyperbolic vistas, peopled by heroes and heroines
we'd mate and slay and *make alive* again.

The glass towers of our *verdopolis* rose like stacked, transparent
threadspools, the hordes we'd amassed clamoring
with anger, with ire, with their own dramatic hungers—
and still we persisted, desperate genii, stoking, accruing,

racing against the gaining morning
and its dismal call to waken;
we climbed all night, as though we might reach again
that infinitesimal aperture, abstract and far-off as heaven,

that once flooded open, implausibly, to bring us here.

FINISHING *JANE EYRE* ON THE
GROUNDS OF THE UNIVERSITY OF
PENNSYLVANIA HOSPITAL

"Reader, I married him"—or so Jane said,
and so I read. *Untrue* was how
this last chapter struck me as I began it,
apocryphal in its happiness

as the white ghosts who moved among us
on noiseless shoes of health, as the criss-
cross of November boughs above
that mocked us as we walked the grounds,

patients cagey in our incendiary
zones, past the sunken pan-pipes
of the laundry's smokestacks,
the barred wards, a family of metal deer

beside the public drive, impaled like cutlery
on the leaf-strewn lawn—and beyond our fences,
rows of mendicant brownstones
and metal-latticed shops beneath a *fuck*-scribbled

platform from which we felt the acrid shiver,
the hellish clank and roar of the el . . .
I carried her here, my Jane, in a still-
unpacked suitcase—Jane, pale root

in the blue corridors of the dormitory,
smallest Jane starving in the fire's outer circle.
Jane beneath the wild plums, the bitter, floral
star of his cigar smoke in her mouth,

disbelieving it, seeing only
the necessity of loss—*"like the necessity
of death,"* but exploding nonetheless: *"I have
as much soul as you—and full as much heart!"*

—and for months, my not eating,
refusing the gym-class, the metal locker
of adolescence, seducing hunger, fucking
thirst, afraid to swallow even my own

saliva, leaving it in pools on the school
linoleum, behind the pew at church, giving
it all back—breasts, eggs, *elán
vital*—an insensate *no,*

Still, I was afraid for *her* to end, my Jane!
And so I slow-pedaled, closed the book
I'd started back in the English class
of my former life, got up and walked

the grounds again, circling, circling,
this time over to the ribs of fence, beyond which,
beneath stripped elms, double-dutching girls
my age saw something—me?—screamed, and fled;

and then the tall, impassive patient
with crossed arms I often passed as I walked
stepped up behind me, saying "You are nothing
but a setting sun," before moving on.

On better days, I wished to be a simple
chair, to hold without feeling.
"Reader, I married him" seemed a phrase
too full, too forgiving for the stark

sentence I was translating, the collapsed
vowels of self, the rickety scaffold of body
caught, like the trees, in a sleight
of sight, all the more *marked*

in a blaze of disappearing,
a death-wish to *be seen*—
I wanted that distinction. Still,
somehow, I unpacked my clothes,

and, one afternoon, backbone to a tree,
read the last chapter through.
It was not so much the marriage,
the baby's black eyes,

Mr. R's miraculous recovery
of sight that troubled me, but Jane's mention
of St. John, her pious, unsuccessful ex-suitor—
why end the book with *him*, why make *his* words

the novel's last—full of a missionary's
self-less zeal for death, his certain reward?
After all, angry Jane was who I longed to be, hurling
a book, missile-shot to the head of a cruel

boor, strange Jane, singing her orphaned
changes over my shoulder, hymns of ransomed
ire, wings of plainness, wings of desire—
Why, then, after risking—and winning—so much,

why end the book with *St. John*,
Arctic loner, exiled by faith?
On a chaperoned outing to the Museum of Art,
I stepped down, buoyed by the plush,

concert-hush of hoarding,
into the catacomb of an Egyptian tomb,
past the gilt carapace of mummies and walls
adorned with men and women contorted in impossible

postures, rendering every part
of the body visble at once so that no stray
appendage, no plate of figs, might be left behind
in the transport to the next life—

and I thought of blue Jane, breaking ice off the basin,
refusing the mirror. Jane gnawing on a stone.
Jane's stricken fugue across the heath,
begging among bees. Jane at the window of health.

Was Jane my angel, then?
Even now, I read but balk to end
her tale, put it down ten times
before I circle around to the last passage

that disturbs me—why?—for its turn
away from love's knit thrall, its redemptive
net—until I remember—it *was* St. John!—who,
practicing duty, lifted Jane, thieved and dying,

from the threshold where she lay, inadmissible,
unadmitted. He *saw* her. And so he haunted her
ever after, implausible and real.
Like my hulking fellow patient,

the stranger who stalked the paths
with me and Jane back in those lost days,
who swerved one day, tilted toward me, seizing
my hands in his huge paws, surprisingly girlish

and soft: "My god," he cried aloud—
an odd, high-pitched child's voice—
"they're the claws of an old woman!"
so that everything in me rose, at last, to defy it.

from BLUE VENUS (2004)

FEAST OF THE VEILED VENUS

That evening on the white bench,
    stars blurring their fates above us
in the blue modalities of heaven,

the hedges heady and zodiacal
    with blossoms, and your eyes closed
a moment, resting: your privacy

could not have been more precious to me.
    What I couldn't say then
I still meant, as when I was a girl

awake under hot sheets,
    watching chain lightning
detonate the curtained temple

of my bit of sky—the bedroom
    window holding emerald Venus
and her consort moon, fool's gold

in a bezel of smoke and mirrors,
    and all around me the silence
of something come and already gone.

I'd twist my legs, restless,
    swathed in covers, into letters—*M*,
V, the number *4*—wondering

if the gist of me resided
    in something I could refuse,
and if it were dangerous

to be too much one person.
    I'd passed through a body
to live in time; by instinct, I sought

an exit through my own, touching
    the wild in me, and free—untamable
as I now know love and truth to be.

INSOMNIA WITH WILLIAM BLAKE

Trembling I sit day and night, ...
To open the Eternal Worlds, to open the immortal Eyes
Of men inward into the worlds of Thought; into Eternity.
                                    —*from* Jerusalem

Sleepless in hodge-podge Soho, lost,
riding my body's bounding outline
through your Infinite London—seeking Liberty—
I chanced upon your house, Saint Blake;
not house—house gone—but concrete steps
and concrete slabs in street-light, black plaque
to mark the place, hosier shop and the roof above
where as a boy you peered into Heaven's
startled Attic, and saw God "in clouds of blood."
And saw Him ever afterwards: an urban beatitude,
a radiant palpable, who visited on the stairs,
at your grate, in Farthing-Pie-House,
and in Lambeth Marsh or in dark of night
at Varley's studio, you crying, "Reach me my things!"
and drunk with vision, fingers sparking
over the copper plates. O graver, translator,
medium constellar and full of larksong:
come to me houseless, with your ink-stained
bread crusts, your woe and your Genius.
Bring your Infant prophecies, your laments,
your trailing wake of personae manifest
and malcontent. And sing, as you did, lustily,
at the last remove, when death ushered you
from one room, into the next. Step here.
Your closed and lambent eyes
are the blue lamps that light my way.

NOCTURNE

Yes, Venus, ripe and undeniable fuse
in the evening wine, I have felt love
fill me with God's furthest time.

I feel it yet beyond this rain-rusted screen,
its metallic sheen pelted by beetles
and the harsh, crescendic ratchetings of the hedge;

further up—there—in the highest, crenellated kingdom
of the old oak, blackly hung—far, far from its roots—
above our tired, obdurate rooftops,

I know it in the lustrous, slow and mating strokes
of the fireflies, in their coded tonguings
of each occidental swag of mistletoe, every bitten branch,

that secret, pelvic recess of stirring leaves.
And though I cannot dwell there, I live
for those illuminated eternities of unharmed hope.

QUEEN ANNE'S LACE

God may doubt our wounds.
But I cannot pass through September's fields—
haunted by the demimonde of your crotched claws,
those tinged and wizened, fisted lanterns
gibbet-hung and scrawled above the goldenrod—
without knowing the swoon—morbidezza—
of your lost and floating world at my thighs,
saucers of negligée, cirrus tatting, flocks of bees
and girlish smocking—attar of clean snow
and shell aureole, cloud-myrrh—
thigh milk—each a chemise cosmos
with its small, shut door of blood.

THE INSOMNIA OF THOMAS MERTON

August 20, 1968: Today, among other things,
I burned M.'s letters. . . . I did not even glance
at any one of them. High hot flames of the pine
branches in the sun!
                    —from Merton's journals

1.

Dream of a maze of footpaths
and the glassy rice fields of Bangkok,
        maps of grass

and water studded by *wats*, enshrined buddhas
                winking with chimerical pondflash
        and cockleburs of gold leaf.

                Toppled buddhas,
        caged in chicken wire and a smother
                of penitential graffiti.

So much burden, so much metaphor,
on the path to grace and evanescence.
No wonder I can't sleep.

2.

In a room suffused with the sad, peppery spice
of marigolds, the Dalai Lama spoke to me
of renunciation, detachment, modeling
the Tibetan posture for meditation, right hand
above the left, discipline over wisdom.
I wanted to speak of *sila*—freedom, grace, gift—

despite being Catholic at the tail end
of a sorrowful year, here, far from home,
where dry thunder talks to itself among hidden peaks
of the Himalayas, and the same constellations stare
whose startling escapements hang above my hermitage
in Kentucky, its little porch opening southeast
toward Aquarius, the Swan's broken wings
above, Cassiopeia over the mountains.

3.

Perhaps M. would remind me,
if she were here, that being alone
and absurd are not things to fear.

Nor is freedom, stepping through
and abandoning selves, until there are no
more steps, I'm homeless, and there's only

the leaping left. *Freedom*, the teacher told me,
is the experience of this leap. I wrote: *I am
the utter poverty of God. I am his emptiness,*

littleness, nothingness, lostness. But M.
was everything, opened places in me, crushed
sweet grass in a hidden yard, shared oceans

with her mouth, made honey with her fingers
and the unclenched crocus of her self.
And she loved me. *You don't*

write poems about nothing.

4.

I am the door,
Christ said. To cross over in perfect
emptiness I must relinquish rooms
I opened, then closed (once, *among other things,*
I burned M.'s letters). Possible to leap here,
perhaps, among thin air and rocks—

       Was it M. I was dreaming
of before I woke, swimming at night
in the green lake at the secret center of my body,
the water a weightless vestment on her shoulders,
waiting for me to call to her from the stony shore,
to hold and keep her, at last?

       How could I have written
among other things?
There is no other thing.

       Dharamsala, November 1968

THE INSOMNIA OF THOMAS EDISON

As the early-evening Metroliner slows
and sidles at dream-flight height
through the apocalyptic back lots
and whistle stops of New Brunswick
and Metuchen and Menlo Park, I think
of the insomnia of Thomas Edison,
awake at 2:00, his cot shoved
against a rack of galvanic batteries
in the gas-lit den of his laboratory.
Some of the men are still at work
on his latest rush of ideas—boiling up
insulating compounds, experimenting
with vacuums—while Edison scribbles
in a notebook another deft, driven ink drawing:
florid, fecund and amoebic improvisations
on his notions for the spiral burner, and the invention
that will become his "big bonanza,"
the electric light. But this is boy culture—
it's not all progress—and a litter of cheap cigar stubs
and sandwich crusts clutters the tabletop
of burners and spectroscopes. It's *paddle
your own canoe*, and late-night pranks—
bets on who can produce the highest voltage
on a hand-cranked generator, guzzling beer
into their black bear mascot, or rigging
an induction coil to the washstand to shock
the German glassblower. And as the train
lurches past the strung-up streetlamps
of outer Elizabeth, each one-legged
in a pool of spotlit asphalt,
I consider the insomnia of the first Mrs. Edison,
Mary Stillwell—whose name Thomas once
dismissively doodled into "stillsick"—alone

for years of nights under her moon-drained
counterpane, a revolver under her pillow,
before she died of "congestion of the brain."
On the verge of night like this, gliding
toward the city through the radiant, industrial
hamlets of chemical plants, past blacked-out
yards of abandoned, blown-windowed, turn-
of-the-century factories, and then, beyond
sumac, glimpses of sub-shops and gas stations
and neon-edged corner bars—passing through
this way, it is possible to believe in coal
and drills and clocks, in the America of grist-
mills, smokestacks, and gears, of escapements
and steam engines—of foundries and forges
and shops—and in our fathers, in droves
from the tract houses, who rode these rails out
each dawn, to the labs and offices
of Westinghouse and General Electric,
Con Edison and Merck,
and then rode them back again each night
to families moored in fragile, incandescent rooms.
There's the skyline now, ablaze and looking—
for all its steepled, invisible rave of technospur
and cyberwave—like the complex, constellar
circuitry of the internal.
I learned in school that the nation
extinguished itself for one dark, full, silent
minute the October Edison died. And here's
the glare-shattered river, the bridge, the strum
and hurtle of light through girders, then the earth,
blasted open to admit and halt us.

NEW YEAR'S EVE

I'm a sucker for a gothic ending:
for example, this opal brooch of sky,
like milk tinged with blood

behind a leaden fret of branches,
the year going down, distant as nursery glow,
natal and passionate.

Returning to my car at dusk
along an alley of tall boxwoods
hiding private yards

—far-off houses, each extinguished
by a certain compromise and sadness,
my tongue stung with champagne

from a party I've just fled,
coat heavy on my shoulders,
reminder that all ways are one, at the last—

my throat stops suddenly with longing.
Not for what I still don't know,
but for what I have known, with you inside me:

blue on blue, and that fierce, white star.
Dark arteries. Splendor of hope's risk,
    still running there.

DOROTHY WORDSWORTH'S INSOMNIA

Such a night, in winter's "Cauld Clash,"
    does not remind one of God:
    cramped, unceiled rafters and newspapered walls,

the scant bedding sepulchral with frost,
    and the one window hung with moon-gilt knives of ice.
    Still, beneath the floor, a starved whisper

of the syke threads below the larder.
    Its tight, arterial run-off from Chummock Force
    taunts with summer's bed of stitchwort

and speedwell, where, in warmer days, we threw cloaks down
    on our fur gown in the orchard ditch—
    my beloved brother beside me—and I was,

as I have always been, "perfectly disengaged,"
    eyes shut to the thrush singing in fits
    and no waterfall above another— . . . *a sound of water*

in the air—the voice of the air—
    and thus it was that William spoke to me,
    without words, of the ardent orphanage of the grave.

This is a hungry margin of the cottage
    to be sure, Mary and William groaning below
    and their children thronging the beds.

Before his marriage, Wm. would read new stanzas to me
    in my bed, or I would pet him to sleep
    with reading "This is the spot—" over and over.

In those first months here, the two of us, alone, my scarlet
        beans throve in droves upon the walls
    and the slow and haw-thorns crowded the bower;

I gladly starched the small linen, washed
        the ceilings a bridal white, spread fresh rushes
    on the flags, hemmed my muslin shifts

by last-light on the garden wall, fingering
        his rusty apple core, digging deep into the night,
    wrists and elbows adrift in lemon thyme as I watched by the moon

for my Darling. But his longing stalked me, like my own,
        and so, at last, having wooed and won a lover for him,
    I moved me to this garret some months before the wedding.

Wm. sleeping badly then, calling out from his room till past three,
        while, all night, on my new window's ledge, the swallows
    that all day twittered and bustled, white bellies

close to the glass, tails forked like fish
        and splayed by building, stole silently in
    and out of their nest, and sometimes rested side

by side, throbbing low to one another
        as the owls renounced sleep
    with a ruthless, mourning motion of their own.

I even gave him poems—the beggar,
        the peddler, the shore of daffodils at winter's end—
    though he did not write what I marked in my journal:

the skeletal deer haunting that golden shore.
    I have been sleepless in winter before: William gone
  courting and me alone, so cold

that day, I had to run twice all the way
    to the foot of the White Moss to get warm.
  That night I slept in Wms bed, and I slept badly,

for my thoughts were full of William—
    and even the Paradise of his unexpected tread upon the stone
  and the familiar motion of my heart imperfectly

re-building itself in that moment—like the swallows,
    their nest a ruined heap of thatches in the yard,
  fallen from the sheer weight of being there together—

even as they began their patient, cheerful
    reassembling, and I saw my own scribbled ledger
  so dismantled, my scrawled accountings

a spectral third to every happy pair—the designated watcher—
    just so my eyes could not help but open,
  so cold were his mouth and breath when he kissed me.

SELF-PORTRAIT

Blandishment of blue
veins in my wrist, I too

am vassal to the heart
with its secret parts

and curtained throne,
its cage of bone

that holds the soul
awhile, above the shadow:

mark of me the sun makes,
then, rising, takes

away—the blue of me—
in perfect verity.

PENANCE I

This sadness feels Medieval,
locked in ice and dusk
with just enough murk

to keep us from telling
two like coins apart
and to send us scuttling home

to the lives we've earned,
with no toothed wheel
in God's clock turret

to mark off and measure
our conflux of gain and loss,
but just enough light left

to blow our souls apart
with loneliness—that hair's-breadth,
secondhand undertaking of the heart.

PENANCE II

Inside my shoes, the sharp stone
   of pleasure shows me the way
my shadow crosses, then disappears

into divinity—mark of me
   absorbed by sun that inches up
the measured hours of my spine,

tenderly, loving each hobbled bone,
   each link and chain,
then soaring beyond the reach of words.

PENANCE III

An early March wind scours
this late afternoon with its annual exposé,

twisting and cuffing a red paper lantern
hung outside the Vietnamese noodle shop.

A runnel from the broken gutter above
taps   taps   against its tissued drum

with a maddeningly slow-motion, lyric clarity,
wresting into itself all of the weak, returning light,

spotting the patch of shoveled snow beneath
with drops of blood. I kick through

the sooty slush, trailing the takeout window
and its sputtering scarf of heat and garlic

behind me. O world that forces joy
upon us, who seemed made for sorrow.

PENANCE IV

What's the penalty
for such a day, spent high

on a crop of stone
overlooking the world's theater?

Even the sky is bright
with the rub of Paradise,

a spectacle below us:
all ransacked clouds and birds

on invisible trellises,
blue shadows roping the valley,

pewter sutures
of river and Interstate,

and sun abstracting the palisades
with pastel bombs of pear and dogwood,

the maple's scarlet wattage,
forsythia's lemon ice,

and my hand at your mouth,
its wet promise—

this makes me feel primitive—
banishing dread and winter's drama.

Perhaps the ransom
is God's to pay, for once,

so we, who have so many
other debts,

can have these hours
for free, night and return

delayed by upheld arms,
hostage and blooming.

PENANCE V

Fare well, stark
   arterial calligraphy
leanly strapping the dead lawn;

goodbye, monastic,
   unimpeded light.
For this gangly impost

of forsythia *will* arch
   beside the drive,
and pollen reign in baroque haze

among treetops
   flocked with gold
and blowsy scepters.

Do we invent what we need?
   Then these clustering birds,
sherry-eyed and exultant scions,

sing for you, from whom
   the world has reclaimed a gift.
Like me, they want to fill your empty arms.

from SATIN CASH (2008)

CRICKET

Apocalyptic knucklebone,
    black-letter font
so antique among the modern things,

you cause the room to flinch
    at my intrusion,
quaver in corners, trill

in mortised triplets the crowded
    heavy boots,
sodden mat, stiff thicket of broom.

Your ceremonial frequencies
    chafe what I might choose
to forget, lonely scrape of a chair

under flourescent morgue-light
    of winter kitchen,
wince as the soul divides.

Hasp of flesh, sear fact
    through which your trespass,
your vesper curfew gnaws.

I CONSIDER MY MOTHER'S MIND

Stars of the Great and Small Bears,
lost in a cobalt padlock above Detroit,
the orient coruscations of car factories,
skating ponds, six-lane highways,
now lumbering across decades
into my childhood suburb, that rimed ruin—
picnic table, dispirited shucks and obeisant leeks
of our winter garden, homunculus
at the mind's edge— I can't return to you,
though I believe you're calling me
from the polar house of hibernal fear
with its skirted vanity table, its angry mirror
& Bakelite brush, bristles up, still fleeced
with a child's hair, a wavering frequency
in the key of oblivion, mammalian, contracting.

THE ICE HOUSE

When my daughter fights on the phone
   with her boyfriend, even her side
of the story unintelligible as my pain—

altering the lit hallway
   between our rooms—I think of the ice house:
pineal, subterranean light,

cave dug in a creek bank among a ganglia
   of ponds, its snug, clapboard dormer
a white-washed disguise

of the wilderness within, winter felled
   beneath corbelled ceiling, slabs of ice
sawn from frozen stream and coulee,

tonged onto sledges, hauled & packed
   among straw, sawdust—so that, in the heat
of rage, or age, or passion,

what shivers of sweet sorbet,
   what unlikely shocks of whine-numbing joy
issue from its galaxy, its dipper.

RENDEZVOUS

The pomegranate fuse
of dusk on the wall

behind you—and you—
within—like a secret side

of the sky. . .
What *do* I believe?

I won't find it beyond
this room.

And when I said *oh, god,*
I was not mistaken.

AFTER JOHN DONNE'S "TO HIS MISTRESS GOING TO BED"

What might she send—a wet sleeve,
or platter of brine-latticed bluefish

dusky with capers, lemons, wine;
a briar for your thumb, a mouth,

lunatic, to suck the blood:
a signal that one too often

inside & now beside herself with thoughts
of you wonders how she might woo

and through dew-whetted keyhole
pursue & sing & win? She is marvelous

with waiting. Come. Hunt here.
Relieve with hands and tongue her heavy hour.

REFRAIN

He says at the ledge
   wait, let's go

more slowly—we listen:
   madrigal breathing,

couched, plush,
   cantleing me,

dressed as with wind;
   & my belonging

to him, especially,
   as with tender pommel,

verge, word, he lifts everything
   I cannot hold

back.

SO

Latitudinal, agonized, this wonder
of shadow on tombstones

plagiarizing willows, hemlock,
tear-strung and haunted.

Winter could not be smaller
in this archive, lawn bee-hung

and alive with flight
lost to suck, to sweet—

to such towering atlases
of azalea and dogwood,

before which, your hand, there—
& why ever leave, why hide,

& why not sing now,
though for so long not,

or, like the wind, insist on a place
for myself in this world?

COLLECT FOR A SEPARATION

Between silence and *yes*,
such distal blues.

I know love is pure
when joy and sorrow inspire

equal gratitude, and yet
these wind-sussed elms require

a certain nineteenth-century attention
today—an eavesdropping.

Even the cool, testicular grapes,
green and cupped in the pergola

beneath wilted purple shade
and a dizzying crewelwork of vines,

waver, heatstruck and speechless
in the solitary séance of my heart.

SYCAMORE TANTRA

Insular majuscule
   of this remnant
scrappy text—scarlet ivy
and copper witch grass
   at the margin of our yards—
I'm on fire for your stuccoed font,
threadbare, friary, stripping
   daringly above the fray,
and all day have watched
you discard your dun
   and ochre clothing
leaf by leaf, each lone raft,
each bit of sleeve, patch of jacket
   settling quietly into the net
of emerald bamboo below—
daring to be—just—*initial*—
   to be left, an elegant,
isolato scribble, inarticulate
and pure, like our bones
   which cannot always
belong to our bodies.

OUIJA

New Year's Eve

Fob, gaud, tinsel
of winter stars,
cosmic bijou:
what am I seeking
when I extend
my soul's *yes yes*
toward you,
brilliant, electrified,
and hopelessly solitary?
What moves me?
Spur of ageless fire?
Astral nadir conspiring
in between?

EMPTY NEST

i.
Pubic tufts, thyme & moss, are greening
    again in the clefts of the wall

latticed by the first flails of warm, late winter,
    and so she removes her shirt

to walk in the garden. Drowsy wasps.
    Velvet, verdigris fontanels

of narcissus, tulip, grape hyacinth
    crown at her toes. She looks down,

face obscured by gauze swagging
    the brim of a wide, straw hat.

Over her left breast, an emerald scar.
    Ink pours from her right,

& in her hand, a heart-shaped stone she carries
    snags the cumulous silks of her skirt.

ii.
She has been dreaming,
wakes in a muslin shroud
of sweat & shadows.
Good. The image is hers—
she can use it in the print shop:
first the amnesia of resin, melted soft-ground
felting the zinc plate, hardening,
then the sharp stylus
cross-hatching the veil,

drawn nipples, swart thatch, no way
at this point to make the milk flow
anything but black, & with each
stroke, piles of zinc filings, eyelashes,
slips of baby nails, tendrils the wren might gather—
a welter of vines, hair, weeds—& the feet
emerging from a drapery of skirt
in annunciation, as then, in gloves,
she flips the exhaust fan, its switch
beneath a red sign, skull & crossbones,
& with lowered mask and metal tongs,
lays the plate in its acid bath.

iii.
Is there someone in the hallway?
    Perfume of her daughter, tangle
of wet hair, smoke, yeasty thread

of wine, her kiss like the other side
    of a prayer, *I'm home, go back*
to sleep, I'll leave the key here,

beside your glasses—
    Ah, so the print-making
was a dream, too. Lucky.

Because she'd forgotten to bevel
    the edges of the plate, to time
the bath, wet the paper,

or how to do a surface roll
     of gold, & also the recipe
for the gesso she'd need to tease out—

from head-drape, bare foot, fisted stone—
     any light within that body
she might call her own.

iv.
The windows slowly turn white—
petri dishes culturing an endless,

filmic loop of new days.
The ravine behind the high school

cradles the vacant whistle
of a passing train, autopsy

of the most lonely cry. Then silence
before the birds. Myopic,

burdened, she reaches across the table,
folded book, cupped dregs of vin blanc,

eyeglasses, to stop the alarm before its reveille,
& of course there is no key.

VINEYARD IN SPRING

The world is prevalent, strained
with the old work of beginning again,

smalt, sexual, congested with blossom;
but here, among lean sorrel fields

scored by cane-trained crosses,
we are novice, tongues fugal

and devout as two mockingbirds
in chevron surplices, flickering

through files of wicker plaits,
gorging in cursive orison, note

mating note, air donning the pelt
of our meaning, the flesh made word.

KEATS HOUSE

Wentworth Place, Hampstead

My blue too lavish—
  what strange powers
Hast thou, as a mere shadow—

for this latticed chair,
  empty lap facing the garden reeds,
lorry surf from the East Heath Road

causing a glass tremble in locked cases,
  comma of your hair pressed
in transparent zeroes burdened as air,

& behind this drape, hung
  from a surveillance camera,
a nimble spider, mica-crumb

envoy from the transient mezzanine
  of fevered, futile spinning.
I gazed until my heart was two.

SABBATICAL

Isn't every convalescence
a childhood, aether hours

provincial in their backwash,
their latent, necessary boredom

of unread pages mottled in shade,
the lenticle of water glass, half-melted ice,

as wasps graze the railing,
hedged currents prickle, swell with blood,

& you sleep in harlequin hammock,
milky raft damasked by mimosa?

Let others wack their weeds, shave
their beards, toil in the barbican

of offices. Nostalgia blushes
behind evening trees. Back-lit swallows.

Is time work? Do even *I* vanish
while you are dreaming?

Beyond memory's damage,
what is this chandelier light,

cogito, without origin, silvering
exquisitely our lengthening hair?

HORIZON

Whose lover is the eye,
traveling where the body cannot.

Who found the word golden.
Who held the prodigal coming & going,

& who, hovering on the landing,
defied the Ratio & sang the copper plate.

Who opened Locke's closet.
Who spent his last shilling

sending out for a pencil—a pen obdurate—
then flew about the room, a Lawless weft

of flame, in all directions—

for William Blake

THE GEESE

Just as God is not my sorrow,
neither does this prow

above our gable where a dream
has died owe me any more than life

has promised us an ending. Though it has.
Is it true the sadder we are, the more things stand still?

Rudder of dusk, perhaps this love
of shape betrays my taste for death.

Even more, I love their going—pioneers—
beyond my knowing.

from VANITAS, ROUGH (2012)

ST. PROTAGONIST

It's bedtime. Tell me a story
as the leaves fly

again, even as we love them
& cannot see them.

Espouser, hero, night errant—
whose wont is to belaud,

chant, cheer, adore
what is before you:

teach me that. The part
in the lady's long dark hair.

The part where that does not matter.
And the ending, sobbed through,

where the improbable becomes
not true, but nonetheless believed.

DEPARTURES: CHAPTER ONE

Morning's mirage, disdainful & calm
    as a mirror,

held the shorn bush that yesterday
    flourished,

now lopped canes & a scant spitfall
    of remnance,

confetti trampled in the clefts
    of vanishing deer.

To touch its truth I punched my fist
    into the chopped molest,

the boscage—withdrew my red sleeve.
    Abstract that.

ST. CHARDONNAY

I have two throats—felted
 intervals.

Call me lonely. Anything
 you like.

No gold quite breaks the dusk
 to smithereens

like self-pity going down
 easy.

Lest this be merely
 a drunken poem,

let a mythic figure sidle in,
 cosmic,

marigolds in the mouth
 & magnificent.

Or worse, bring on her lesser
 coz, Empowerment. Ha.

Two throats & each a sacred force.
 But who would want

to talk about that.
 To talk at all.

MIDAS PASSIONAL

No one has touched me for weeks,
yet in this drugged, gilt afternoon, late,

when nothing is safe, I'm paralyzed,
as though so wildly desired—passing solo through the garden's

cinnamon, marigolds, famished roses, where a matted shingle
of the swept-up human hair I begged from a local beauty shop

& spread out fruitlessly among the blooms & thorns
to keep away the deer might well be a satyr

passed out in the palace's candied gold—
that something regnant with a strange, god-like power

could not help but reach out from the umbral blue
to tap my white arm. It is a day to die,

the light autoerotic, theatrical, with an unbearable listing,
stalled in cusp, in leonine torpor. Is courage artifice?

As though to answer were within my means.
Or to even move my mouth.

GOLDFINCHES

If never was the question. Even then.
That *when* feels closer now

might embarrass me before this window,
more mirror than I would like at this hour,

bathos of years ghosting face, throat,
my impatient turning off of the lamp.

Now I'm small again, and the world outside
mysterious, perfumed, & large.

Were I not to feel this, would now
be when? I watch the primal arousal:

day's lost fruit stoned by black hills,
the metafucked in the metaphysical, &c.

Then five duskal flames assign me
the barkless dark, the barren cherry.

STILL LIFE WITH HARE & KNIFE

When the witnesses sent their children,
mother was skinning rabbits.
What else to do,
pamphlet extended,
but call for her? Salvation! Watchtower!

Hands like maple leaves turned,
around the corner she came,
knife hung loose.
Coral reef of souring crabapples,
blue sky vitals, the cool paste of the brochure

as she cursed
the quailing clot of grown-ups retreating
in church coats, spectacles, booklets clutched
like shields as they shoved their brood behind them,
backed away. She cursed them again

and again, sending the innocent to do
their dirty work. Long white feet,
the rabbits had
given off heat. On the picnic table,
they stiffened in a halo, gnats, mosquitoes

that bit me too, the rapture
transfused. What did it mean
to save or be saved
as acorns struck & webs appeared
overnight, child-sized, spangled, shrouded knots of dew?
Did it have to kill you?

VANITAS, ROUGH

In a panel of floor-propped mirror
your tongue in me is mine, too,

glass pear of the toppled goblet,
drunken wasp grazing semen yolk

of split, glazed oyster shells,
Death blowing soap bubbles

out the orbital sockets, glycerin
filming a halved walnut,

taut brains of meat a tinged pink
tulip petal falls toward

just as I rear up into stomp
of opened drawer, a third, raptor's eye,

blue-ish, topaz egg, already rising
in the drenched, heaving wilderness of our face.

DEBT

This stable dawn, unplated,
shows me the world without me,

a different predicament from jealousy—
three players, one bed.

Your heart speaks of it in dactyls—
even the waters will close one day—

despite the pelvic altar, our share
of rented air, stairless landing

hiving our hair, like these trees, louche
with taboo green that lingers despite

the blooded syntax of exit.
Which even death cannot prove.

CHRISTMAS STOUP

Ink slurs into byssal threads,
   split blue caskets of mussels
scapular in ritual archipelago, butter, cream,

the chowder pot a holy trencher
   on a night stour, bitter
with advent, wilted cruxes, tarragon,

bassinet of clamshell, shucked,
   fragile saddlebags,
houses primeval: slughead, mantle,

foot, all vulnerable, indomitable.
   Frozen tongues lengthen magnetically
at the cornices. The moon. Ah, the moon,

a cameo unspendable, the world
   in verbless fugue state, triad of thyme,
bay; the sorrowful sea by the body unlocked.

TRAILING MARY & MARTHA: 3 AM

Difference—had begun—
        —Emily Dickinson

Outside, unfathomable barking.
Within, I'm quandary, a drupe

stapled by bees, a sink full of mastic plates.
An erotic scenario? The truth is

a prayer once saw you inside me;
how dare your absence now adjure

that fastening? That dog again.
Behind glass, trucks in gear-lust

jaw dumpsters in the cul-de-sacs
& I consider Dickinson in the sink room,

limestone chink of dinner dishes,
forks tuned against an enameled basin,

noon fracturing the room.
That figure in the doorway—

why not travel with him now?
The God-gene, of course;

expensive to know for whom we minister,
for whom we wake & sing.

ST. BRONTË

When does one's beloved become a concept?
Maître, I wrote. Intelligence continues

despite a headache. Seed thrown
from the stoop to birds, winged hunger.

I am unable. To not—.
I am in want. Thank you for not

sending facts. Which would break me,
jealousy with its sister exotica.

Here: morning milk, its mortification.
The kitchen's a stable.

Rooms bloom inside me I can't enter.
At least not specifically.

The failing is mine, no doubt.
To abstract is to surrender.

St. Hope. St. Story. Is syntax erotic?
If so, please. Please read. Here.

GOD'S GYM

In blunder of dusk I negotiate rush hour
past the strip-mall fitness center,

plate glass tableaux of bodies in treadmill
silhouette, an elbow in the signage above gone dark.

I can hear from here the earbuds stair-stepping,
bottomless techno sham, no bridge, no left hand,

& consider the fit of cherry blossoms
that blew against my blouse this morning.

You sent them to me;
also the cursive plum branch in ghostly waver,

blue jay already swallowed by white sky. Lover,
I could say, or little brother, consider the Shakers,

their simple holes and pegs complicated by glossolalia
of twitch and stomp *as if you had a thousand years*

to live, and their celibate shafts of conversion,
as if you were to die tomorrow

of adoption, the upper room of the heart emptying
into tongues of esophageal fire.

THE IRISES

for Charles Wright

A fly quizzical among tufted causeways,
blue sudden avenues spumed overnight from spears.

O silk, my throat closing around a sob.
That fly again, minute leaden tank, thread-hooves,

busy, busy, to whom I mean nothing.
Relief in this. Yet to me he's singing beside the dugout, the ditch,

cosmic with pathologies. A grave matter,
that perfume—father, mother, son, & daughter—

those phrases—no hands, no feet, how else depart,
eyes opened without ceasing—

why I can't disturb their bruised hymning,
why I gather them all inside, until I'll know—

BLACK SNAKE

Does this longest day define me,
sleepless as I always am with solstice qualms,

white, extreme stagger of light refusing
to depart bamboo, amethyst contusion, the yard

across which I drag a garden hose?
From an open upper-story window

a recording of that ululating indie harpist girl,
my daughter's new favorite singer, shrieks

in faux child-voice of harts and velvet
prisons. I want to like her music,

but instead it makes me want to gnaw rocks.
Apricot pendulum lyre ticking

in the locust, blue fieldstones
of the crumbling fence, old crush

on the world whose beauty I've always feared
to see directly—will that leave me, too,

despite years that never brought me the weightless
grace I thought I'd become for myself, or anyone?

I hope not, bending to the spigot
that suddenly moves, uncoils, all my years

rushing like ebony water around a pier
then bellying off into the dark, wanting nothing.

FRIDAY MOTET

Day ends, chainlinks the subdivision,
its unspeakable splay

vying with shiver from stadium lights
igniting the high-school soccer fields,

stropping the rooftops & bird-bridled bamboo
with a cleansing flame. *Eleven, twelve,*

fourteen, twenty!, a boy cries, uncovering his eyes
in the fields, and from here: dusk, scrambling,

shrieks in broom sedge, the gasp
of their fathers' beer cans opening in porch shadows,

one of them saying, *Man, she fucked. . .*
she something me. . . something, something. . . ,

sense lost as I mouth evening prayer—
"you who are worthy at all times to be praised

by happy voices"—into the opened window.
Last night, my friend dreamed of his death,

a tumor in his mouth, under the tongue he used
to speak into the receiver, telling me

"This is my last poem." When we end,
will it be as when, for private reasons,

we live gloriously in one another
for an hour, more, as long as we are given

—not criminal, but moored, like these vines—
kudzu, honeysuckle, belts unfleshed

& undeniable with incensed horizon,
a reason to bear lying down apart?

DEAD MOTH

In every lonely place,
    an altar,

gulf between adjective
    & noun, uncurling,

pale green in stiff thumbnail
    sarcophagus, mica sheen.

Time wasted, & worse, looms,
    as a bit of the reverend

dark road, why say very right,
    breaks off, upheaves,

unfolding despite last light,
    despite light.

HIBERNALPHILIA

Triangular glasses, brumal volts, gin,
frescade of pearls, plucked, sunned olives,

grave albino onions, juniper nip & the cusp of snow,
we sip slow, as at a glacier's lip. Holy day.

I'm thinking fingerbone salad, the marginalia
of Emily Brontë, intricate skeleton keys,

not blade but the pierced heart, the bow
to which torque must be applied.

That blue note of exile in your eyes.
Meeting mine you say *The way you inhale*

semen oysters rosewater ordure of armpit, footsole,
I smell time. I meaning you. You smell time.

Alone along the Interstate, later, runnels rapt into ice,
sun sinks, aguish, an amber smut, ruttish

behind black roofs, crotched ridge.
Why miss any chance to be changed?

I'm ready, you said, back in our niveous cups,
gelid narcotic by which I mentally undressed you.

You called my drink *chaste*. The intoxication
love brings when we mean to gladden,

mouths boreal and high. Terrified, beautiful.
Unashamed. They are the same.

AFTER THE MEETING, A RED FOX

If ever more ravened, junked, numb-sconced
I could not recall it, sopping in aftermath

dusk's blossom bock, ink-musk ale
at rusted window screen, the annual carnival

a neon embolism blurring the horizon's black seam
that from the brine of my dispirits

struck me as the portajohn & ticket-littered
portal of hypocrisy and the soul's mojo shutting down.

Then you, scrabble in the bamboo,
fluent rapacious pelt, burnt, elegant-booted streak

flecking the despond no longer just mine
with a shiver estival that—even as language cages

it now, a loping scriptural and starving—
every word of it I winged to you then a barbarous traveling.

from OREXIA (2017)

THE WISHBONE: A ROMANCE

Never to belong again to wings
    that lifted, to heart,
to blood's forsaking bodice:

this lyric forceps,
    felled flèche d'amour,
furcula picked and dried

with earthy feints of sage
    & fused with remnant gristle—
clavicles tongued, now thumbed,

memento mori
    of a hard year. Why not,
then, after giving thanks,

break it, too—
    talismanically? What good
is loss starved forever after?

To keep from freezing,
    even a priest might commit
the Virgin's statue to the flames.

TEMPLE GAUDETE

Deus homo factus est
Natura mirante.

Is love the start of a journey back?
If so, back where, & make it holy.

St. Cerulean Warbler, livid blur,
heart on the lam, courses arterial branches,

combing up & down, embolic,
while I, inside, punch down & fold a floe

of dough to make it later rise.
Recorded Medieval voices, polyphonic,

God has become man, to the wonderment
of Nature. Simple to say: there is gash,

then balm. Admit we love the abyss,
our mouths sipping it in one another.

At the feeder now. Back to the cherry, quick,
song's burden, rejoice, rejoice.

O salve & knife. Too simple to say
we begin as mouths, angry swack,

lungs flooded with a blue foreseeing.
Story that can save us only through the body.

OWL HOUR

Houseless against gray glower,
juniper dank, grisaille pagoda firs,

& sounding an unplumbed sleeting
within, girlhood's obscure guilt lingering,

a voice calling you inside, this betiding
fur-stirred wedge in high oak, jacketed child,

prehistoric eye in unlikely presiding
above the park's trapeze of empty swings.

I know it will disappear
if I look away. To be clear,

Figment, seed invisible in pent snow:
any mutiny in this going is mine, I know.

BAROQUE HOUR

In which death yields to style:
ruddled vista humping intricacies

of vines, twinings tombed & calligraphic.
Is this distortion possible only in lies,

folds, the enigmatic golden stall
prose gnaws the edges of—

this cedar nave blooded by sundown
suddenly become all my self,

one doomed syllable, like *young*?
Unlike infinity, which has no native tongue?

CELIBACY 1

Unmarried, the heart ejaculates
what it must, scarlet-purled, arterial,

away, away. Or conversely, married,
it requires all—venous, freighted with waste.

Fuck the heart. On the radio,
driving home, I learn the Brits

are into all things Scandinavian.
Sunlit schools, bare breasts, the Aurora Borealis.

A "scandi trance." Maybe. Ice is a mystery
of whatever blue enchantment swiped

my view this morning. This is no allegory.
I'm north of myself these days

with a fist full of silver keys
I lose every night in my dreams.

CELIBACY 2

Nervous, twigs split, become swallows,
jeté the platinum poring chits

over the mountain's bistered tinge.
Is a murderer secreted in each one

of us, someone we once knew,
even embraced in a mirror

without premonition? No way
this season knows it's ending.

Instead of "murderer," let's say "orphan."
You're leaving, you say? Either way,

what to do from here to then,
when language means to stay?

TEMPLE AGE

Sycamores phrasal, ashen,
strap, bi-chromatic,

this cross-hatched patch of woods.
Respond with hard answers, please.

My season is upon me.
Green in there somewhere, yes,

even red, if I hash around?
Goodbye beauty, I might also say.

Depart loveliness, at last.
Passing by pallid fields,

I confess I dreamed of us.
Precarious weeks, these,

that never want me small.
Or parceled. Rather all.

HARE

As light fails, despite ceaseless rain,
she comes, for my phlox, cotton lavender,

doused & two-dimensional, apprehending world,
whatever that is to her, in the slight tremor

& pinch of flank, the one eye
rolling in hazel truckle, feral, desolate,

the other wayward, gazing who knows where,
in mated gambol or placid trench of lilies, flares,

or across the lawn's green sea, vitrine lens to you,
traveled afar, under grapevine, above a bowl

of oil & blue heap of scraped shells, reading.
Always the tug between what touches (the wine,

salted lips, fork, tongue, lapped napkin),
& what looks. She's hungry. I want to defend

what I think I've grown. How see each other
except through this knowledge?

The sodden yard, the minute sudden snails:
to see something whole, must we make it small

the beloved a pupil in the eye? This creature
constructs, in the scale of her scribbling heart,

an ancient mind: a private, besieged chamber
that dilates a hair's breadth, you to remember.

OREXIC HOUR

My body, made to be entered
& exited. Almost wrote "edited."

Eaten. Odd to be so direct.
Who cares that the maples blistered

with renewal today, at last,
despite shackles of snow,

not for me, not for you,
obeying an instinct akin to human,

but not. Still freighted
by the gadget of a self, I admit

I care. Is it my appetite for this violent
flux—crocus mons afloat beneath oaks,

stamen odor, bulb-aroused mouth—
that, against effacement, I invent?

TRUST HOUR

The rust in it.
The hard-wired rigor mortis,
knee-jerk, historical.

You are suspicious,
Heretic, of slack nostalgia.
Denial, jealousy, & such craft.

The instant of "no choice"
occurs, tea-maker says,
when there is just one need:

boil, steep, serve.
Your hand over my heart
shows me shape

of cup. No formula
except suffer, sip, swallow.
Gladden. Drink again.

READING JOHN CLARE, HEADING NORTH

Vermont Studio Center

Going alone, with song for company,
homeless at home, homeless at home,
though sometimes time drops from the shoulders,

into hedges with low, darting creeps,
escape-ways, & who are we then.
Skirting the Labour-in-Vain public house,

eating grass to humor hunger.
Getting up as famished as you lay down,
O gipsy, pilgrim in fugue state,

on the lam from Lunacy,
trekking a long way only to be locked away again
"after years of poetical prosing."

Gravel in the shoes recalls the body
to every soul chasing ignis fatuus,
Friar's lantern. *I'll bend down for a dime,*

St Charles Wright said. *I won't for a penny,*
but I will for a dime. In truth, I'm traveling
not on foot, but by air, minute crosshairs

sketching the coast's asphalt amalgam below,
then opening, lowering over green loping
switchbacks capped with ice.

How large a shadow wings must make
caping small things hidden
in another story. A second spring here,

swards in flush, long purples, blue-bottles,
peepers craunking, a red mill shouldering the river,
its small crescent of rapids. Rush and throstle.

"I am in a Mad House & quite forget your name
& who you are," wrote Clare, but also, "I can be miserably happy
in any situation, in any place."

As he was, watching starnels swarm at dusk,
waiting for Death to bring the bill.
Same day, another bed, we're never beyond the right of seizure.

The moon a flipped coin winking in the water's scrawl,
marked with our names though not a word spoken,
riding the sweet black tongue to the falls.

THE WHALES

Belied, be-laired, in sleep's massacred vista
of blood that is the sea within,

like a god, entranced from above,
I felt the whales before I saw them, gorgeous

foetal continents, lost, glistering, parental,
mare-blue beneath sediments of stellar silks,

planktal glass, moving the wrong way
up a narrowing, inland stream.

With all my blindness, I wept
to save them, mysticeti, their kimono lobes,

pharyngeal bells, and lonely spume,
their homesick crying like a scarf of fox grapes

reaching sailors still hundreds of miles
from land. They placental. They

in four-chambered beyonding.
And my own heart, beached—erupting

into hollow room, to closet door,
to clock face, where I failed

and failed again to help them
over the rhapsodic rasures of this world.

ACCIDENTAL

Broken mantle clock, squat turreted castle
kept for its hand-painted closet,

coiled beehive in gauzy umlaut of wings,
gilding pale as the heat the vagina gives off,

after—. After what? An afterthought, now,
to change "vagina," for modesty's sake,

to "portal to this world." Truth is, the key
signature of any day's measure can be altered

of a wild sudden. How a deleted "i"
turns another word to "marred," for instance.

Bond indifferent as a dish of untouched soaps.
Shaped like eggs, no less. What is it

floods our clothes in the muddled dusk
of our beginnings? Is it what's inside the door

of the flawed clock, a fury of shadows
cast by nothing? Fluke or fate,

whatever happens or doesn't happen,
the portal happened once. To make you,

you who were an I. To make me,
the child you were. You what I will be.

TEMPLE TOMB

John 20: 11–18

In this marrow season,
trunks tarnished, paused,

I am garden. Am before.
Asleep. Then the changes:

placental, myrrhed. Wet hem
when you appeared.

What did your body ever have
to do with me? In my astonished mouth,

enskulled jawbone guessed,
though as yet I didn't know you.

You sprung. You now intransitive,
tense with heaven.

Gardener, which of us said do not touch.
Which one of us was undressed?

MOREL PATCH

Ghetto miraculous,
   tipsy monastery, mysterious

embroidery erupting rashly
   in thatch beneath the dying ash,

gnomic roofs of steep snows,
   bee skeps on hollow stems, blown

honeycombed tutulus
   with whiff of kiosk,

cloister, old world side-show
   trousered intimacy, glass-blowers,

or the throat swollen in filigree
   by a swallowed key, or bee:

intoxication, bell whose knell
   or tonic only time can tell.

MY FATHER'S DREAM OF THOREAU

What shall I learn of beans or beans of me?
Henry David Thoreau, *Walden*

He doesn't know it, but he's in the long row
with Thoreau, decades behind him, boyish soul

in old body bent over an ancient tool,
Johnson grass & crab already whispering *fool, fool,*

claiming, impatient, the mile he's just hoed,
craven moon above glistered as the needle's eye

his dead wife mouths, whiskery tail of thread,
linsey-woolsey stitching of bean plants moth-eaten by deer

that step behind him, soundless, this time a doe
and two new fawns in voracious flow,

tracks labial in the fresh chop. Why do it, then,
so much more than he can ever salvage, eat, or share,

well past eighty, though the holes he makes, in cindered din,
are not for himself to lie down in. A catch of rain

hums farewell in a notched gauge; netted by stars,
wasp-gouged pears drop, surreptitious,

a visitor's foot-fall coming from the orchard
whether he's ready, or not. How then can our harvest fail,

Henry calls back to him, cheery, hale,
in the nineteenth-century voice

of his father's father, also a farmer, when a furrow
has never cared one whit for its husband?

DUET

New Year's Eve

Two sisters side by side,
benched at the gleaming fin

of the living room's out-of-tune baby grand,
work out a mash-up, Adele's "Hello"

& Kate Bush's "Wuthering Heights,"
Hello, it's me . . . , Heathcliff, it's me, it's Cathy,

voices by turns treble, then cemetery-dusked,
meandering, & hungry

as the sinew-tracks of moles
sponging December's yard,

painted mouths of iced puddles,
branchless leaves snaring the window

with inhuman gale.
One swallows this heavy beauty,

rolls the mordent perfume
back to bloom as the other slips out

of autumn's whalebone stave, descant.
They sing as if still girls. As if before

love's scarlet evidence, & not, like the year,
the trees, already moved, moved through.

TEMPLE ON MY KNEES

When this day returns to me
I will value your heart,
long hurt in long division,
over mine. Mouth above mine too—
say you love me, truth never more
meant, *say you are angry.*
Words, words we net with our mouths.
Soul is an old thirst but not as first
as the body's perhaps,
though on bad nights its melancholy
eats us out, to a person.
True, time is undigressing.
Yet true is all we can be:
rhyming you, rhyming me.

HOW I MIGHT SOUND IF
I LEFT MYSELF ALONE

Turning to watch you leave,
I see we must always walk toward

other rooms, river of heaven
between two office buildings.

Orphaned cloud, cioppino poppling,
book spined in the open palm. Unstoppable light.

I think it is all right.
Or do tonight, garden toad

a speaking stone,
young sound in an old heart.

Annul the self? I float it,
a day lily in my wine. Oblivion?

I love our lives,
keeping me from it.